# J for
# Jordan

An Alphabetic Journey

**By: ESRAA GHAZO**

**Illustrated by: AURA**

# A

A is for Amman the capital city of the country.
It is like a swan in love poetry.

# B

B is for a Bedouin scarf. Red and white. Giving a bright sight. Held by a circle of black rope. You put it on the top of your head, called Iqal.

C is for a Cup of Coffee. You should shake it from side to side. Believe me, it is a guide; otherwise, we will keep on refilling it, if you do not mind.

# D

D is for Dinar, the currency of Jordan.

1 Jordanian Dinar = 1.41 United States Dollars.
And both have the same green color.

E is for Export. It is a clear port for some support. Jordan exports potash, phosphates, vegetables, and clothing. Yes, I am not joking.

F is for Falafel. A street food snack. Made from chickpeas with a special smack.

# G

G is for the Gulf of Aqaba. Where the Red Sea is.
Feel free to swim and glee.

# H

H is for Hashemite. Jordan is known as the Hashemite Kingdom of Jordan. You are right; Hashemite is derived from Hashemi. Such majesty with sweetness blending, directly descending, all the way back that you will track to Prophet Mohammad (Peace be upon him).

المملكة الأردنية الهاشمية

**HASHEMITE KINGDOM OF JORDAN**

I is for Independence. Jordan gained independence from the United Kingdom on May 25, 1946. Hooray, after the darkness of pain, we have seen the dawn of gain.

**J** is for Jordan. Where I was born. Breath of home. The land of love that you should roam.

K is for Kingdom. Jordan, ruled by a strong king manages all things. Abdullah II bin Al-Hussein is the king of Jordan.

11

L is for Land. A different kind of sand. Count on your hand;
Jordan's total land area is 89,342 km².

M is for Mansaf. Our national dish. I wish you enjoy it with no rush. Lamb cooked in yogurt sauce. Yay, I am the boss. Served with rice. That is so nice.

N is for Nature. Jordan is a combination of different features. Sand, deserts, and a lot of green places. See all the beautiful faces.

O is for Olives. Green and fresh.
Ready for picking in October.
The year is almost over.
Eating and processing into royal oil.
I am so loyal to this soil.

P is for Petra. The red rose city. It is so pretty.
Along the Siq, dim and pearled. One of the Seven
Wonders of the World.

Q Q is for Queen. Where have you been?
Waiting with the crowd to see our Queen.
Rania Al-Abdullah is the Queen consort of Jordan.

# R

R is for a Royal Anthem. The Jordan National Anthem is AS-SALAM AL-MALAKI AL-URDUNI.
Can you see? The Jordan military band singing our royal anthem, with a TV crew following them.

S is for Salt. The Dead Sea in Jordan has 9.6 times more salt than the ocean. It will not be understood as they are spoken. You should visit it and describe your emotion.

T is for Thob. The Jordanian traditional dress. A wide variety of embroidery prints and joyful handwork. Wow, it makes me shine, so close to mine.

# JORDAN

الأُردن

U U is for Urdun. Have you ever heard of the Arabic word for Jordan? It is Urdun.

V is for View. Petra, Wadi Rum, Ajlun and Um Qais too. All claimed to be the best views in Jordan.

W W is for Wadi Rum. A desert with red sand where the rocks will proudly stand.

X

X is for OryX. Arabian oryx is the national animal of Jordan. White with straight horns. Pride like that of the morns and a shoulder bump, raise your tiny thumb.

# Y

Y is for Yogurt. The main ingredient of Labneh. Do you want a quick snack? It is bread with labneh. Do not forget to form it into a dough and bake it up nice and slow.

Z is for Zayt and Zaatar. The main dishes are from Jordanian cuisine. Guaranteed to keep you lean. I like the scene with the color green.

Made in United States
Orlando, FL
13 September 2023

36899800R00018